FOR THE MOTHER WHO HAS EVERYTHING

A Funny Book for Mothers

TeamGolfwell and Bruce Miller

For the Mother Who Has Everything, Bruce Miller & TeamGolfwell

FOR THE MOTHER WHO HAS EVERYTHING, A Funny Book for Mothers, Copyright © 2022, Pacific Trust Holdings NZ Ltd. All rights reserved for the collective work. No part of this book may be reproduced or transmitted in any form, or by any means, electronic or mechanical, including photocopying, recording, or by any information storage and retrieval system, without written permission from the author, except for brief quotations as would be used in a review.

This is the second book in the *For People Who Have Everything* series.

Cover and Images are from Queen Graphics or Creative Commons

ISBN 978-1-99-115652-5 (Ingram Spark Paperback)

ISBN 979-8-40-515663-7 (KDP Amazon hardcover)

ISBN 979-8-40-515484-8 (KDP Amazon paperback)

ISBN 978-1-99-115658-7 (Ingram Spark EPUB eBook)

Boring? "Somebody said that being a mother is boring. That somebody never rode in a car with their teen who just got a driving permit."

-- Unknown

Mothers. "Mom, thank you for your friendship, love, support, and undying devotion. You made me what I am today."

Mom replies, "Thanks sweetie, now go wash your hands, they're filthy. Comb your hair and turn out the lights. Do you think I own the electric company?"

Eagle eye. One mom was amazed at her son, "My three-year-old wears his clothes inside out, put his shoes on the wrong feet wearing only one sock, yet he can spot a Brussel sprout or a tiny piece of onion on his plate from 12 feet away."

For the Mother Who Has Everything, Bruce Miller & TeamGolfwell

Mrs. Germanotta's advice to her daughter Lady Gaga. "Stephani, try not to be so reserved."

-- Unknown

The influence of babysitters. Overheard, "My dad has been helping to watch our kids during the pandemic. Now my one-year-old gestures and shrugs like a 61-year-old Russian man."

Humbling. "Kids humble us. The other day on a flight home my daughter, Olympia, insisted on running up and down the aisle, and when I finally got her to sit still, she threw up all over me."

-- Serena Williams

How true. Why is it that my 10-year-old daughter is totally wrong on most things and yet I haven't ever won an argument with her?

Puzzling and funny. Does your 6-year-old ever mouth the words instead of saying them out loud when he uses Zoom? I suspect he purposely wants to make you think there is something wrong with your unmuting function.

Mom's phone message left on her daughter's phone.
"If you need to be picked up from soccer practice, let me know. If this is a true emergency, and you're bleeding, call 111 and tell them to call me. If you need me to call and cancel your violin lesson because you didn't practice, do that yourself."

-- Unknown

Where did she go? After closing on a new home, mom was busy unpacking with the house in a complete mess and dad was at work. Suzie, their three-year-old kept asking to go to the nearby playground.

"Sorry, it's raining out. Mom is very busy, and I'll take you there soon."

That somehow didn't seem enough of a reason for Suzie who was bound and determined to get to the playground. So, she slipped out the door and walked to the playground located about halfway down the block.

Luckily a neighbor's mother, an elderly Polish lady noticed the little girl walking in the rain and followed her.

Once Mom realized Suzie wasn't there, she ran out down the block only to discover Suzie going up and down the slide, and the elderly lady was sitting on the bench, and both were laughing away and totally oblivious to the rain.

An "exceptional" mom. "Today I ran 5 miles, cleaned the entire house, taught my youngest the alphabet, cooked a delicious dinner, and put the kids to bed sound asleep before bedtime. It is exceptional what you can accomplish when you lie."

-- Anon.

A clever way to get a wake-up. One mom asked another mom how she managed to get her sleepy-head son out of bed in the morning.

"I just put the cat on his bed." She replied.

For the Mother Who Has Everything, Bruce Miller & TeamGolfwell

"How does that get him going?" the other mom asked.

"The dog's already there." ☺

Stylish mom. True story. A new mother was getting her baby ready to go with her to the grocery store and she had her long scarf hanging down from her neck. As she was putting the baby in the car, she wrapped one side of the scarf around her neck thinking she was now looking like a highly stylized and sophisticated mom with a two-month-old.

What she didn't realize was one of her boy's diapers was hanging down her back and she walked around the store like that until a stock boy said, "Ma'am, I think you've lost something."

The better you are. "But kids don't stay with you if you do it right. It's the one job where, the better you are, the more surely you won't be needed in the long run."

— Barbara Kingsolver, an excerpt from "Pigs in Heaven"

For the Mother Who Has Everything, Bruce Miller & TeamGolfwell

After birth. "No one told me I would be coming home in diapers too."

-- Chrissy Teigen

Glad that you're my mother

"I'm glad that you're my mother

Kind and caring and strong,

Coz surely no one else,

Could put up with me this long."

-- Holly Giffers

Lots of kids. Mother Teresa once said, "How can there be too many children? That is like saying there are too many flowers."

Feodor Vasilyeva and Valentina Vasilyeva had 69 children – sixteen pairs of twins, seven sets of triplets, and four sets of quadruplets – between 1725 and 1765, a total of 27 births. 67 of the 69 children were said to have survived infancy. The claim is somewhat disputed as records at this time were not very well kept. Valentina died at the age of 76 and Feodor had another 18 children with his second wife, who had 6 pairs of twins and 2 sets of triplets, making him a father of 87 children in total. There is more data about Feodor's children in the Guinness Book of World Records. [1]

In a more modern example, Mariam Nabatanzi from Uganda had 44 children (43 survived infancy) by the time she reached the age of 36. There were 3 sets of quadruplets, 4 sets of triplets, and 6 sets of twins, all apparently due to a rare genetic condition causing hyper ovulation. In 2019, at the age of 40, she underwent a medical procedure to prevent any further pregnancies. [2]

By the way, it's reported Genghis Khan fathered over a thousand children from a large harem of women he whom he captured or acquired in some other way, reaching numbers of about 2,000 to 3,000 women. Scientists in the Russian Academy of Sciences estimate he has 16 million male descendants living today in Central Asia. [3] That would be a very confusing Father's Day for Genghis getting cards from places he'd hadn't ever been to?!

"You'll be fine," said the paramedic as Mom is being taken away by EMS. She moans, "The last thing I remember was my family was trying to cook and do the dishes…"

Her four-year-old son is saying as they cart her away, "I tried to make coffee, but bad things happened!"

Seven-year-old daughter is saying, "The pancakes DID NOT WORK OUT. I cannot stress that enough!"

Husband is saying, "I asked her not to go into the kitchen…"

– Unknown

"Hey! Mother of five!" A husband, so proud of the fact that his wife had given birth to 5 children, begins to call her "Mother of five" rather than by her first name.

The wife, amused at first, chuckles when she hears it.

A few years down the road, the wife has grown tired of her husband's worn-out description.

"Mother of five," he would say, "Get me a beer!" Or "Hey mother of five, what's for dinner tonight?"

The annoying phrase persisted to a boiling point.

Finally, while attending a party with her husband, he jokingly yelled out, "Hey mother of five, I think it's time to go!"

The wife seized the moment and shouted back, "I'll be right with you - father of three!"

Only one day off a year? "Yes, we call it Mother's Day, but technically and practically, you still have to work that day."

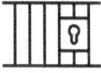 -- Anon.

Supermodel mom. If a mother's stress burned more calories than normal, mothers would look like supermodels.

A mother's unusual dilemma. I've read where one mother wondered whether she should be more concerned about her son who locked her out of her bedroom, or the other son who taught her how to pick the lock.

Tired mom: "If I manage to survive this week, I would like my straight jacket in hot pink and my helmet to sparkle."

– Unknown

Young moms choosing names. "My mom had me when she was 15, so I know the younger the momma, the more jacked up your name will be."

– Finesse Mitchell, Actor, author, and comedian

Helping God. "God could not be everywhere and therefore he made mothers."

– A Jewish Proverb

Mi casa, su casa. "I told my mother-in-law that my house was her house, and she said, 'Get the hell off my property.'"

– Joan Rivers

For the Mother Who Has Everything, Bruce Miller & TeamGolfwell

"Nobel Prize for Mothers"

Mom you are a shining star

Though the world doesn't know your name.

You have no fancy title

Like Baroness or Dame.

Mom you really are a star,

My mother, mentor, and friend.

A Nobel Prize for motherhood,

Is what I'd recommend!

And if I won the lottery

I'd share my win with you

I'd take you Mom on a spending spree

Each day the whole year through!

For the Mother Who Has Everything, Bruce Miller & TeamGolfwell

You may not be famous,

As your face is known to few.

But Mom I think you are wonderful

And I'm so proud of you!

-- Unknown

Driving with mom. "You ever drive with your mom as an adult? I would rather pick up an escaped convict. At least they're satisfied. My mom, she doesn't really say anything out loud, she just makes that noise that moms make when they think they're about to crash, which is roughly every 10 seconds."

-- Gary Gulman

A mother's eyes. "A mother's eyes are like God. Impossible to get away from, they see everything."

-- Matshona Dhliwayo

"I am free." A mom asked her 4-year-old son to stop yelling.

He replied, "I'm not yelling. This is my normal voice. I've been whispering all my life now I am free."

-- Anon.

A mother knows things no one does. Mothers know things others don't have any idea about. For example, one lady says her mother, or any mother for that matter, is just the person to contact to find out how long chicken lasts in the refrigerator. Books won't help you know that as only mom knows your habits, refrigerator model, the store where you bought it, etc. You need hands-on experience to know these things.

An easy birth? "Don't tell your kids you had an easy birth, or they won't respect you. For years I used to wake up my daughter and say, 'Melissa, you ripped me to shreds. Now go back to sleep.'"

-- Joan Rivers

Complicated stuff. "I've conquered a lot of things. Blood clots in my lungs – twice. Knee and foot surgeries, winning grand slams after being down match point – to name just a few. But I found out by far the hardest is figuring out a stroller."

-- Serena Williams.

True story. After mom put her children to bed, she changed into a worn-out top with beat-up jeans and began to wash her hair. While washing her hair she heard her children getting restless, noisy, and giggling too much for bedtime. So, mom wrapped a towel around her wet hair and rushed into their room and settled them down with severe warnings.

While going back to the bathroom, she heard her three-year-old say, "Who was that?"

-- Anon.

Automatic attitude adjustment. "It is not until you become a mother that your judgment slowly turns to compassion and understanding."

-- Erma Bombeck

A loving toast to mom. "Raise your glass for all the magnificent moms in our lives!

"I mean for the amazing mothers, grandmothers, godmothers, stepmothers, mothers-in-law, foster moms, bonus moms, other-mothers, aunts, wives, partners, sisters, friends, fellow moms, mentors, and all women who love with a the one and only and ever-loving mother's wonderful and infinite loving heart."

-- Anon.

Leonardo DiCaprio. Did you know that Leonardo DiCaprio was named Leonardo because his pregnant mother felt his first kick while she was viewing a Leonardo da Vinci painting in an Italian Museum? [4]

Can't get that stuff off easily. Is it true that Michelangelo's mother is reported to have said, "Mike, why can't you paint on walls like other children? Do you have any idea how hard it is to get that stuff off the ceiling?

Like mom like daughter. "I like to talk to my mother every single day because hearing how delusional I may become one day makes me appreciate every day I have left with my sanity."

– Tami Vernekoff, Comedian

Oldest Moms. The oldest woman to conceive naturally, according to the Guinness Book of World Records, is Dawn Brooke of the UK. She became the oldest woman to conceive naturally giving birth by Caesarian section in 1997 at the age of 59 years. She managed to ovulate past her last period. [5]

The oldest mom to give birth by IVF treatment is Maria del Carmen Bousada Lara who gave birth by Caesarean section to twin boys, Christian and Pau, at the age of 66 years 358 days at the Sant Pau hospital, Barcelona, Spain on 29 December 2006. She was not married. She passed away 3 years later from cancer. [6]

The oldest mom to give birth to her grandchild is American, Jacilyn Dalenberg, who was a surrogate mother for her daughter, who carried and delivered her own grandchildren. She did this for three grandchildren for her daughter and all three were girls in 2008 in Cleveland. [7]

The oldest woman to appear nude in Playboy magazine was the famous Mamie Van Doren in 2006 when she was 75 years old. [8]

Realistically speaking. "I always say if you aren't yelling at your kids, you're not spending enough time with them."

-- Reese Witherspoon.

Changing diapers...help! The average Mom will have changed approximately 7,300 diapers by the time her baby reaches age two! [9]

Thinking of having more than one child? Think again! One mother was concerned and felt it was highly important to put parents who have only one child on notice that you should first give it a lot of thought before deciding to have another one. She is reported to have said this while she was splitting a chocolate M&M in half.

Yes, one M&M candy piece…

In half…

Unique. "A mother is one who can take the place of all others but whose place no one else can take."

– Cardinal Mermillod

Wait till the baby cries. A joke. With the help of a fertility specialist, a 60-year-old grandma has just delivered a baby. All her sons, daughters, and grandchildren come to visit to meet the newest member of their family.

When they ask to see the baby, the 60-year-old grandmother says, "Not yet."

Shortly later, they ask to see the baby again. Again, grandmother says, "Not yet."

Finally, they say, "When can we see the baby?"

And the grandmother says, "When the baby cries."

So, they ask, "Why do we have to wait until the baby cries?"

The new mother says, "I forgot where I put the baby."

Thank you is not enough, Mom. "She's a king, a queen, a warrior, a woman, a leader, a rebel; my mother, my teacher, my bestie, my partner, my inspiration, my mommy… 'Thank you' is too weak of a word! I celebrate you every day!"

– Alicia Keys

Chinese Proverb. There is only one pretty child in the world, and every mother has it.

-- Chinese Proverb

"There is only one Mom." The teacher wants her students to express their love to their mother, so she asks them to create a sentence with the phrase "There is only one mom".

It's the first student's time, and he answers the teacher, "My mom always tells me stories and gives me a kiss before I sleep, so I love her. There is only one mom!"

She seems like a nice mother," says the teacher. She then points towards another student, "It's your turn now."

"I had a cold last week, and my mom took care of me. She gave me medicine and made me hot cocoa. There is only one mom, so I love her!"

The teacher smiles and then asks Little Jon to create his sentence. "Well," he began, "My mother was watching TV yesterday, and she wanted something to drink. She then asked me to grab three beers from the fridge. I went to the kitchen and opened it, but there was only one beer. So, I said her, 'There is only one, mom!'"

It's time! The longest pregnancy ever recorded lasted 375 days, nearly 100 days longer than a normal pregnancy. This was due to placenta previa where the condition is such that the baby develops slower than usual. She finally gave birth to a healthy 8-pound baby boy. [10]

The shortest pregnancy was 21 weeks 4 days and the newborn baby girl weighed only 410 grams at birth, and she survived and remains healthy today. [11]

Show me. Napoleon's mother is reported to have said, "All right, Napoleon. If you aren't hiding your report card inside your jacket, then take your hand out of there and prove it."

Toddlers. "May your coffee be stronger than your toddler."

– Unknown

Making room. Typically, the mom's uterus grows from the size of an orange to the size of a watermelon in the last trimester. [12]

How did Mother's Day begin in the US? A lady named Anna Jarvis (1864 – 1948) held a Church memorial service in 1908 for her mother in West Virginia honoring her mother three years after her death. That caught on super quick as within the next 5 years every state in the US held a memorial service for mothers. President Woodrow Wilson then signed Mother's Day into law as a National Holiday. [13]

During the 1920s Mother's Day became commercialized by the greeting card and the floral industry which did not sit well with

Anna Jarvis. "A printed card means nothing except that you are too lazy to write to the woman who has done more for you than anyone in the world. And candy! You take a box to Mother—and then eat most of it yourself."

Due to the heavy commercialization, she tried to undo it all and have Mother's Day revoked until she passed away in 1948 trying to preserve her original intention to honor mothers without commercialization to no avail.

There is an International Mother's Day Shrine in Grafton, West Virginia, honoring the first Mother's Day that Anna started in 1908 that has been designated as a National Historic Landmark. [14]

Cleaning. "Trying to clean your home while the kids are home is like trying to brush your teeth while eating chocolate cookies."

– Anon.

Home Security. "Good luck robbing my house," one mom said. "My home security system is LEGOs on the floor with perhaps one or two Hungry Hippos!"

A child's eyes. "In a child's eyes, a mother is a goddess. She can be glorious or terrible, benevolent, or filled with wrath, but she commands love either way. I am convinced that this is the greatest power in the universe."

— N.K. Jemisin, The Hundred Thousand Kingdoms

Dumbwaiter. The definition of a dumbwaiter is a waiter who asks the children if they want dessert.

Amy got busy. Amy Schumer married Chris Parker in February 2018 and after the announcement by Prince Harry and Meghan Markle that they were having a baby, Amy photoshopped Chris Parker's and Amy headshot over a picture of Harry and Meghan and she jokingly announced, "Chris and I are thrilled and I'm almost positive he's the father. I look forward to competing with Markle every step of the way."

Easy? "It's not easy being a mother. If it were, fathers would do it."

– Betty White, The Golden Girls

Be yourself. "My Mom is a fierce warrior that would surrender her life for anyone. She encapsulates the essence of a woman ready to conquer life the way it should be lived. She is pure, accepting, wildly courageous, filled with love for most everyone. She is a beautiful glow that holds you when you sleep, fighting the enemies in your dreams. She is my best friend. Thank you, Mom, for giving me the confidence to be myself, always."

– Jessica Simpson

What's this bill? Goldilocks' mother is reported to have said, "I've got a bill here for a broken chair from the Bear family. Do you know anything about this Goldie?"

Silence. "Silence is golden unless you have kids, then silence is suspicious"

For the Mother Who Has Everything, Bruce Miller & TeamGolfwell

– Nicole Fornabaio

Best Mother's Day Present. Three very wealthy brothers are arguing over who got their mom the best Mother's Day present.

The first brother says "I got mom the best gift! I bought her a brand-new house! It's so huge, its practically a mansion!"

The second brother says "Not even close! I got mom the best Mother's Day gift! I bought her a brand-new luxury car, and I even hired her a chauffeur to drive her around! She just has to tell him where she wants to go, and he'll take her there in her nice new car instantly."

The third brother says, "My gift is the best one! Mom has always been very religious, so I bought her a priceless pet parrot trained by the church to say any bible verse! If you just tell the parrot the book, chapter, and verse number it will be able to recite it from memory!"

A few weeks later, each brother gets a letter from their mom regarding their gifts.

To the first one, she writes, "The new house you bought me is too big. I only need one room to live in, yet I spend my day cleaning up the entire house."

To the second one, she writes, "I'm too old to go many places. So, the car and chauffeur just sit in the garage doing nothing all day."

To the third brother, she writes, "Your gift, I liked! The chicken was delicious!"

One-handed. "Becoming a mother makes you realize you can do almost anything one-handed."

– Unknown

What are you eating?

Child: "Mom. Mommy?

Mommy, Mommy, Mommy…

Mommmmmmeeeeeeee.

Mommeee, Mommeee, Mommeee, Mommeee, Mommeee…

Mommmmmmmmmy, Mommy, Mommiiiiiiiiii…

Mom. Mom. Mom, Mom. Mom. Mom. Mom. Mom. Mom, Mom. Mom. Mom. Mom. Mom. Mom, Mom. Mom. Mom. Mom. Mom, Mom. Mom. Mom…

Mom, what are you eating?"

Mom: Valium.

A mother's heart actually does grow. Figuratively and literally, the minute you found out you were expecting, you may have felt like your heart grew three sizes. The funny thing is, it really grows during pregnancy — maybe not three times as big, but still. Your heart must pump even more blood to support the baby's development, so it bulks up a bit. [15]

Don't mess with mom. (Airline names and numbers are fictitious) While taxiing at the exceptionally busy London's Heathrow Airport, the crew of a United flight departing for Miami made a wrong turn and came nose to nose with a Continental 777 airliner.

The lady controller who was a hard-working single mom knew how to handle this, "United 3671, where the HELL are you going!? I told you to turn left on Alpha taxiway! You turned right on Charlie! Stop right there! You don't even know your alphabet! Get it right!"

She didn't stop there "You stay put! Don't you move a millimeter! You've created quite a mess! You will get further instructions in half an hour and in the meantime, you stay right there! You got that, United 3671!?"

"Yes, we do ma'am," one of the humbled crew replied.

The ground communications fell silent afterward. Others listening understandably were giving the ground controller time to calm down.

After a long silence, an anonymous pilot pierced the silence and said, "You wouldn't be one of my ex-wives, would you?"

Month of May

For all the diapers

that you changed,

For the Mother Who Has Everything, Bruce Miller & TeamGolfwell

For all the playdates

you arranged.

For all the trips

back and forth to school,

For cleaning all the spit-up

and the drool.

Why is there only

one Mother's Day?

You should have at least gotten

the ENTIRE month of May.

-- Anon.

Sharing. "Nothing is more satisfying than the sound of my husband trying not to lose his mind while the kids give him the same behavior, they've been giving me all day. Marriage is about sharing. I'm a mom who likes to share."

-- Anon.

Joy. "Being a mom is one of the biggest joys of my life. I have learned so much from my three kids...patience, kindness, humility, creativity and of course, and how to tell a great knock-knock joke! To my wonderful kids, I love you more than you will ever know (You will figure that out as soon as you have your own kids). Always know how grateful I am every day I get to be your mom!"

-- Reese Witherspoon

Greek God. Gaia, or "Mother Earth", was the first goddess in Greek mythology. She created herself out of primordial chaos. She also created the Earth and the universe.

Cleaning your son's room. A mom was cleaning her son's bedroom when she found a load of serious bondage gear & fetish mags.

She asked her husband: "What do we do?"

Husband said: "I'm no expert, but I wouldn't spank him!"

"Al, you must look good for the picture." Albert Einstein's mom is reported to have said, "But, Albert, it's your senior picture. Can't you do something about your hair? Styling gel, mousse, something?"

The Silver Plate. A mom visits her son for dinner who lives with a girl as a roommate. During his meal, his mother couldn't help but notice how pretty his roommate was. She had long been suspicious of a relationship between the two and this had only made her more curious.

Throughout the evening, while watching the two interact, she started to wonder if there's more between him and his roommate.

Reading his mom's thoughts, his son volunteered, "I know what you must be thinking, but I assure you, we are just roommates."

About a week later, his roommate came to him saying, "Ever since your mother came to dinner, I've been unable to find the silver plate. You don't suppose your mother took it, do you?"

"Well, I doubt it, but I'll email her just to be sure!" He sat down and wrote,

"Dear mom,

After you visited me, the silver plate has been missing. I'm not saying that you did take the silver plate from my house, and I'm not saying that you don't take it, but the fact remains that it has been missing ever since you were here for dinner.

Love,

Your son."

Several days later, he received an email from his mother which read,

"Dear Son,

I'm not saying that you do sleep with your roommate, and I'm not saying that you don't sleep with her: but the fact remains that if she was sleeping in her OWN bed, she would have found the silver plate by now, under her pillow.

Love,

Mom"

I marvel. "I marvel at you. It's so hard to put into words EVERYTHING you do. And you do it with such grace. Thank you for giving the greatest gift of love and continuing to show what it means to be a good person in the world. You make me realize how much my own Mother has done for me."

-- Justin Timberlake on Jessica Biel

Metaphor: Child: "Mom, what are metaphors?"

Mom: "This house is a disaster area. My life is a train wreck."

Child: "I know. but what is a metaphor?"

Understanding feminism. "I grew up in a world where authority was female. I never thought to call myself a feminist because of branding. I had this skewed idea of feminism. I thought it meant being a woman who hates men. Later I read Chimamanda Ngozi Adichie's 'We Should All Be Feminists, I was like, "Oh, this is what my mom taught me. This is simple. I don't understand why everybody is not like this."

-- Trevor Noah

Hi Mom! Must call Mom on Mother's Day! There are about 122.5 million phone calls on Mother's Day in the US, making it one of the busiest phone days of the year.

You know you're a real mom when…

"Walking down the aisle of a department store alone feels like a vacation and going on vacation feels like work."

"You get up at 7am and feel like you've overslept."

"Picking up a person and smelling their butt feels both necessary and normal."

"Happy time is their nap time."

"Conversing about poop is normal and necessary."

"It takes longer to get out of the house than it does to do your errands."

"You are home on Saturday night, and you don't mind."

"Your fantasies are about sleeping."

"You go shopping for yourself and only come home with bags full of things for the kids."

"You tell your boss you'll be right back to work on that important project after you go potty."

"Your idea of world peace is when everything has a drive-thru."

"You're shocked when you slept through the night."

"Doing things with two hands feels like a luxury."

"All you want is some alone time and then miss the kids as soon as you get it."

"Silence is golden, unless you have a toddler, then you know you must get up and find that toddler right away."

"When you turn on Netflix and automatically turn on cartoons before realizing your kids have been in bed for an hour."

"When the floor in your car is covered with cheerios, goldfish, and some unrecognizable gunk, but you are always too tired or too distracted to care.

"They also say it's a sign that you are a mom of 2 or more kids when you watch your child eat a goldfish off the floor and don't even blink."

"When you are in such a rush you shave the same leg twice and when you realize it, you just shrug and leave the other one hairy."

"When you find random pacifiers and toys in your pockets, purses and drawers."

"When work counts as your social life."

"When you're hiding in your bedroom to eat a chocolate bar because just for one time you don't want to share any of your food."

"When you have no money for yourself but thousands to spend on little surprises for them, then being fully satisfied by the happiness in their eyes."

"When your child throws a tantrum in the store, stiffens like a board so you can't buckle them in their car seat, goes limp as you try to get them in the house while carrying bags in the other hand… and then, while tucking them in at night, they hug you tightly with chubby arms. While you watch them close their eyes, they look at you with such love, that you forget and forgive the day."

The first 12 months. "We spend the first twelve months of our children's lives teaching them to walk and talk and the next twelve telling them to sit down and shut up."

-- Phyllis Diller (1917 – 2012) American stand-up comedian, actress, author, musician, and visual artist.

Steadfast prayers.

"Mom. Thank you for all your steadfast prayers for over 32 years, thank you for your sacrifice, thank you for your intelligence, thank you for wit, thank you for your undeniable positivity and keen intuition.

Thank you for raising 3 fantastic children that really love you (TBH I'm the black sheep and most annoying one). I know I can always call on you and you will be right there even if I just need a pet and a spoon. I am so blessed.

Love,

Your feather/turtle/bird."

– Katy Perry

What does your mom do? We were sitting around talking about what our parents do for a living and one guy said, "My Dad works for the post office but my mom's a Hydroceramic Engineer."

Everyone was impressed until someone said, "Oh, she's a dishwasher?"

Voice tone is important. Mom (happy voice) "Okay, kids, it's time to go now."

20 minutes later. Mom (Darth Vader voice), "I said, let's go."

Record for heaviest baby. According to the Guinness Book of Records, Anna Bates was a tall woman of 7 ft 11 inches. Her husband, Martin Van Buren Bates, was also over 7 feet tall.

Anna gave birth to a boy weighing 9.98 kg (22 lb.) and measuring 71.12 cm (28 in) at her home in Seville, Ohio, USA, on 19 January 1879, breaking the record for both heaviest birth and longest baby. The baby, who was not officially named but just referred to as "Babe", sadly died just 11 hours later. There is another report of even a heavier baby was born by an Italian lady named Carmelina Fedele in 1955. Her newborn weighed 22 pounds 8 oz but was not documented very well. [16]

A new perspective. "Having children just puts the whole world into perspective. Everything else just disappears."

– Kate Winslet

Male-dominated pastry. Q. Why are there "poptarts" but no "momtarts?"

    A. Because of the pastryarchy.

First Lady. "At the end of the day my most important job is still mom-in-chief."

    – Michelle Obama, American attorney, and author who served as the first lady of the United States from 2009 to 2017.

After they leave the nest. When mothers talk about the depression of the empty nest, they're not mourning the passing of all those wet towels on the floor, or the music that numbs your teeth, or even the bottle of capless shampoo dribbling down the shower drain. They're upset because they've gone from supervisor of a child's life to a spectator. It's like being the vice president of the United States.

    – Erma Bombeck

Cabby. A mother and her young daughter were visiting New York City. The mother was trying to hail a cab when her daughter noticed several wildly dressed women who were loitering on a nearby street corner.

The mother finally hailed her cab and they both climbed in, at which point the young daughter asked, "Mommy, what are all those ladies waiting for by that corner?"

The mother replies, "Those ladies are waiting for their husbands to come by and pick them up on the way home from work."

The cabby, upon hearing this exchange, turns to the mother and says, "Ah, c'mon lady! Tell your daughter the truth! For crying out loud! They're hookers!"

A brief period of silence follows, and the daughter then asks "Mommy, do the hooker ladies have any children?"

The mother replies, "Of course, Dear. Where do you think cabbies come from?"

Transformation. "My favorite thing about being a mom is just what a better person it makes you on a daily basis."

– Drew Barrymore

Bull####? "I'm very lucky to be pregnant, but this is some bull####." Amy Schumer posted when she just learned she was having a condition called hyperemesis gravidarum that is characterized by severe nausea, vomiting, weight loss, and more electrolyte disturbance. It's more than standard morning sickness.

Mr. Rogers. Every sweater that Mr. Rogers wore on his well-known TV show was hand-knitted by his mother.

The one and only Rodney. "When I was born, I was so ugly the doctor slapped my mother."

"When I was a kid, I got no respect. I told my mother, I'm gonna run away from home. She said, On your mark."

"One time my whole family played hide and seek. They found my mother in Pittsburgh!"

"My mother had morning sickness after I was born."

"When my old man wanted sex, my mother would show him a picture of me."

– Rodney Dangerfield (1921-2002) American stand-up comedian, actor, producer, screenwriter, musician, and author.

Oprah's view. "I believe the choice to become a mother is the choice to become one of the greatest spiritual teachers there is."

– Oprah Winfrey

Amy Schumer on birth. "I am so happy squeeze the sweetest, giant skull out of my tiny precious…and most likely take a dump in front of five doctors and my lover. I just want to steer clear of sharing overly personal details."

– Amy Schumer

No more bull####. After her first child, Amy Schumer, now a respectable married mom and wanting to change herself from a very funny single lady to an exemplary mom said, "That's right, I'm done saying dirty things. It's just not who I am anymore. I know it's pretty weird to hear that from me but get used to it because I'm basically already kind of an amazing mom."

Hi mom! How are you? Restaurants are busier than any other day of the year on Mother's Day with about 90 million dinners served on that day. There are over 150 million greeting cards sent on Mother's Day and it is celebrated in almost every country in the world.

Cleaning house. "Cleaning your house while your kids are still growing is like shoveling the sidewalk before it stops snowing."

-- Phyllis Diller

Frat house. "Having children is like living in a frat house- nobody sleeps, everything's broken, and there's a lot of throwing up."

For the Mother Who Has Everything, Bruce Miller & TeamGolfwell

--Ray Romano

Dating the right man. "I once dated a guy so dumb; he could not count to 21 unless he was naked."

-- Joan Rivers

Only a mother knows this. "I loved you before I knew you."

-- Anon.

Working moms. In some countries like Bulgaria, working moms get a one-year leave plus a little over half of their salary during the first year after having a baby, and fathers are also entitled to 37 weeks of parental leave.

In Cuba, new moms get 6 months maternity leave with full salary and there are many countries with massive time for maternity leaves with pay. [17]

"I promise not to get angry". A mother and her teenage daughter go shopping and walk into a clothing store. Mom selects a dress and decides to try it on. Mom walks out of the dressing room wearing the new dress and asks, "Does this dress look good on me?"

The nervous teen replies, "Mom, you promise that no matter what I say you won't be angry?"

The mother smiles and says, "I promise."

After a brief pause, the daughter replies, "I'm pregnant."

Motherhood takes patience. "Motherhood takes patience, understanding, persistence, practice, humor and a lot of moist towelettes."

– Anon.

"I found life". Mom to her child. "I gave you life, but really, you gave me mine."

– Unknown

Tom Hanks. When Tom Hanks was a boy he acted in a Church play, and the night of the first performance, he, unfortunately, forgot his lines. His mother was sitting in the front row trying to prompt him. She gestured and formed the words silently with her lips, but it didn't help. Tom's memory was flat-out blank.

Finally, she leaned forward and whispered the cue, "I am the light of the world."

Tom beamed and with great feeling and a loud clear voice announced, "My mother is the light of the world."

Bad investment? Hugh Hefner's father worked as a public accountant, and when Hugh, as a young man, asked him to loan him money to start his magazine, he turned him down telling Hugh that a magazine is not a good investment.

His mother, however, took Hugh aside and gave him a thousand dollars from her own savings to help him.

Mom's influence. "Sometimes I open my mouth and my mother comes out."

– Unknown

A mother's wish. "I want my children to have all the things I couldn't afford. Then I want to move in with them."

– Phyllis Diller

First word. Mom talking to her baby, "Say Dada."

Dad: "Don't you want her to say Mama as her first word?"

Mom: "No way. The other two give me no peace, this one is yours."

"Say Mama" "From a phonetics standpoint, it's much easier to say 'mama' than 'dada.'" Scientists have advised that "More babies say "Ma" as their first word mainly because it is easier to say by simply opening and closing the mouth. For that matter, the word for mother begins with an 'M' sound in almost every language." [18]

Think you know love? "Just when you think you know love, something little comes along and reminds you just how big it is."

– Anon.

Full Heart. Motherhood: "If you think my hands are full, you should see my heart."

– Unknown

"Everyone should have kids. They are the greatest joy in the world, but they are also terrorists. You'll realize this as soon as they're born, and they start using sleep deprivation to break you."

-- Ray Romano

Ideal Mom. "I'd like to be the ideal mother, but I'm too busy raising my kids."

– Unknown

A mother's advice to her children. (Brief excerpts from "Slammed")

"Find a balance between head and heart."

"Push your boundaries, that's what they're there for."

"Don't take life too seriously. Punch it in the face when it needs a good hit. Laugh at it."

"And laugh a lot. Never go a day without laughing at least once."

"Never judge others. Know good and well how unexpected events can change who a person is. Always keep that in mind. You never know what someone else is experiencing within their own life."

"Question everything. Your love, your religion, your passions. If you don't have questions, you'll never find answers."

"Be accepting. Of everything. People's differences, their similarities, their choices, their personalities. Sometimes it takes a variety to make a good collection. The same goes for people."

"Choose your battles, but don't choose very many."

"Keep an open mind; it's the only way new things can get in."

"And last but not least, not the tiniest bit least. Never regret."

"Thank you, my children, for giving me the best years of my life."

"Especially the last one."

— Colleen Hoover, from Slammed

For the Mother Who Has Everything, Bruce Miller & TeamGolfwell

The doctor is amazed. A mom takes her daughter to the doctor and the doctor asks, "Okay, what seems to be the problem?"

The mother says, "It's my daughter Suzie. She keeps getting these cravings, she's putting on weight and is sick most mornings."

The doctor gives Suzie a good examination, and then turns to the mother and says, "Well, I don't know how to tell you this, but Suzie is pregnant. About 4 months would be my guess."

The mother says, "Pregnant?! She can't be, she has never ever been left alone with a man! Have you, Suzie?"

Suzie says, "No mom! I've never even kissed a man!"

The doctor walks over to the window and just stares out of it.

A few moments later, the mother says, "Is there something wrong out there, doctor?"

The doctor replies, "No, not really. It's just that the last time something like this happened, a star appeared in the East and three wise men came over the hill. I'll be darned if I'm going to miss it this time!"

Roll with it. "It is truly a blessing. But I'm going to be tired for the rest of my life. When you're up at 3 o'clock in the morning, and they pee on you, you just have to smile."

– Wanda Sykes

Men are necessary. "My mom told me the only reason men are alive is for lawn care and vehicle maintenance."

– Tim Allen

It's your turn. The Daily Mail reported the average woman takes two minutes and five seconds to change a diaper, while it takes the average man just over a minute and a half. So, moms, if you're pressed for time, call in dad (but make sure he knows what he's doing and does a great job!). [19]

Single mother. "Being a single parent is twice the work, twice the stress and twice the tears but also twice the hugs, twice the love and twice the pride"

-- Unknown

A new role. Comedian Mayim Bialik was remarked as her children got older, "I'm used to whipping out carrot sticks like they're a six shooter," she said. "I'm used to putting Band-Aids on boo boos. I'm used to nursing away hunger and pain and fear... Like, I'm used to being the most important person in their lives. Now I'm a presence in a new way."

Teaching your child. "A child can be taught not to do certain things, such as not to touch a hot stove, not to pull lamps off of tables, and not to wake Mommy before noon."

-- Joan Rivers

Guinea pigs? I have read where some feel working mothers are guinea pigs in a secret scientific experiment to show that sleep is not necessary to human life. Makes you wonder, doesn't it?

For the Mother Who Has Everything, Bruce Miller & TeamGolfwell

Mom's humor through tough times. "I see your sense of humor finding its way into some of what I now know were extremely trying times. You made all of it fun. You made all of it an adventure. You are our rock. No matter how big we get, you're our mom. This Mother's Day I am seeing things a little differently. One day our kids will look through albums and flip through memories of their childhood. I hope it's as colorful as what you gave me. Thank you, Mom...for all of it. We love you so much."

-- Nikki Reed

Riddle. What do structural walls, and moms have in common?

A.   They are both load-bearing.

Mom kept Christmas. "When my British-Church of England mother married my Canadian-Jewish Father the deal was that she would embrace Judaism, but she wouldn't give up her Christmas tree. So, I grew up with Christmas every year. I loved it then and I love it now."

-- Hilary Farr

Saying no. "Someday, when my children are old enough to understand the logic that motivates a mother, I'll tell them: I loved you enough to bug you about where you were going, with whom and what time you would get home. ... I loved you enough to be silent and let you discover your friend was a creep. I loved you enough to make you return a Milky Way with a bite out of it to a drugstore and confess, 'I stole this.' ... But most of all I loved you enough to say no when you hated me for it. That was the hardest part of all."

-- Erma Bombeck

Logical. "Give me a sentence about a public servant," asked the teacher to her 3rd-grade students.

One small boy wrote: "The fireman came down the ladder pregnant."

The teacher took the lad aside to correct him. "Don't you know what pregnant means?" she asked.

"Sure," said the young boy confidently. 'It means carrying a child."

Selfless love. "Thank you for showing me what selfless love, generosity, compassion, kindness, power and strength is. Thank you for bringing my perfect brother and sister into this world. You have taught me to love everyone the same and keep my eyes open to the ones that don't. I love you so much...I am so lucky."

-- Bella Hadid

Single moms. "She has to have four arms, four legs, two hearts and double the love. There is nothing single about a single mother"

– Unknown

Superior smells. During pregnancy, women have a superior smelling ability that may even make you feel like vomiting. Some believe that is your body's way of assisting you to avoid foods you shouldn't eat. [20]

Want more than two kids? "Oh hell no. You don't let them outnumber you. There's two of us, there's two of them. That's it!"

For the Mother Who Has Everything, Bruce Miller & TeamGolfwell

-- Wanda Sykes

Amazing. In 1997, Bobbie McCaughey from Iowa gave birth to the most surviving children from a single birth at that time. She had the first surviving set of septuplets (4 boys and 3 girls).

Later it was reported a 27-year-old woman gave birth to the world's first set of surviving octuplets in 1998. Nkem Chukwu, from Houston, gave birth to 5 girls and 2 boys by Caesarean section. The other child, a girl, was born two weeks before.

In the summer of 2021, a woman broke the world record by having 9 surviving babies. They were born in Morocco and "the family said they go through 100 diapers and six liters of milk in a day. And the couple already has a daughter." [21]

Don't be pushed around. "One of the greatest pieces of advice I've ever gotten in my life was from my mom. When I was a little kid there was a kid who was bugging me at school and she said 'Okay, I'm gonna tell you what to do. If the kid's bugging you and puts his hands on you; you pick up the nearest rock...'"

— Johnny Depp

Said no mom ever. The American Academy of Pediatrics generally recommends a good balance between screen time and physical activities. Also, being in a pandemic is no excuse for excessive screen time.

One stressed-out and lockdown mom reported she has made the difficult decision to limit her children's iPad use to no more than say, 14 hours a day and she hopes you do the same.

How many? Currently, American moms have an average of about 2 kids. Back in the 1950s, they had an average of 3.5 kids. Way back in the 1700s, they had 7–10 kids. But today in two states, Utah and Alaska, moms on average have three children.

The month when most mothers give birth in the U.S. is August, and the most common day for birth is Tuesday. [22]

Groceries. A son asked his father, "Dad, do you know the difference between a pack of cookies and a pack of elephants?"

"No." Dad replied.

"Then it's a good thing Mom does the grocery shopping!"

Roseanne. Roseanne Conner starred in her well-known TV series "Roseanne" and for the first time, the series showed Roseanne as underpaid, barely able to control her children, and overweight. It also showed a mother who led the household, and her TV personality was very popular. The TV show and Roseanne's character were highly successful and did not depend on her appearance. [23]

Learn laughter. "The first person I learned I could make happy with laughter was my mother, whom I idolize. It was a powerful thing to realize. I knew I had found my life's work."

-- Ellen DeGeneres

Believe in yourself. "Wishing a very Happy Mother's Day to this special and beautiful lady. You taught me to believe in myself. I love you."

-- LL Cool J on his wife

Great cook. One boy asked another, "Does your mom make you say a prayer before dinner?"

"No, my mom's a great cook!"

Prodigy? "My daughter knew her alphabet and could count to 15 a little after she turned two. Everyone told me she was advanced for her age, and I began having visions of my very own Doogie Howser.

"She's about to turn three now, and yesterday I watched her try to put on a tank top as if it was pants for twenty minutes. I guess she'll be my little Rain Man."

— Nathan Timmel, Comedian

What? A famous eyewear store announced they are offering free glasses on Mother's Day for all mothers for the eyes in the back of their heads.

Feedback. The definition of feedback is when the baby doesn't appreciate the strained green beans.

Immediate good behavior. Ever notice the unnatural fake-forced and excellent behavior of a child when the other child is being sternly corrected by mom's raised voice?

Not easy. It's not easy being a mom. If it were, dad would be doing it.

-- Betty White

Do I still have chores? "I had Bar mitzvah -- it was just me and my mom. And she's celebrating. And she's reading things to me in Hebrew. I don't know what's going on. And she's telling me that now I'm a man. And I'm like, does that mean I have no chores? And she's like, no, you still have chores, but you're a man."

-- Trevor Noah

You trusted me and my crazy goals. "When I was a li'l nugget you trusted my desires of some pretty insane goals. You believed in me...and I am so blessed to have you as my mother. It would be an honor to be half as much as the woman you are when I'm older."

-- Laurie Hernandez, US Olympic gymnast, and a member of the U.S. women's gymnastics team dubbed the "Final Five" at the 2016 Summer Olympics. She ultimately won the U.S. gold in the team event.

I took your advice mom. Do you remember these? They are old worn-out sayings you swore you wouldn't ever tell your own children.

"Money doesn't grow on trees you know."

"Close the door! - were you born in a barn?"

"Because I said so."

"If so and so jumped off a bridge, would you jump off a bridge?" (I took your advice Mom. Yesterday, they all jumped but I didn't).

"Stop crying before I give you something to cry about!"

"Your face is going to freeze that way."

"Hold your horses."

"I'll wash your mouth out with soap."

"When I was your age - I had to walk 5 miles to school in snow in the freezing cold."

"You're not made of sugar, you won't melt."

"Elbows off the table."

"Just wait until your father gets home!"

"You'll understand when you are a parent."

"Oh, and who do you think you are? The Queen of Sheba?"

"Come home when the streetlights come on."

"I wasn't born yesterday."

"Hey is for horses."

"Put a sock in it."

"We're not laughing at you; we are laughing *with* you."

"Wipe that smile off your face or I'll wipe it off for you."

"Don't you make me pull this car over."

"Don't put that in your mouth. You don't know where that's been."

"Life isn't fair."

"Don't get smart with me."

"Go ask your dad."

"Always wear clean underwear in case you're in an accident."

Never alone. "When you are a mother, you are never really alone in your thoughts. A mother always has to think twice, once for herself and once for her child."

– Sophia Loren

Grandparents. The definition of grandparents is people who think your children are wonderful even though they're sure you're not raising them right.

Magic Genie. Mom was cleaning the garage and dusting off very old lamps and a beautiful young lady genie suddenly appeared who said, "Thank you for releasing me as I have been in the bottle for many, many years."

Her husband heard the strange voice and rushed into the garage and was totally amazed to see the gorgeous genie.

The genie continued speaking. "You appear to be a wonderful couple and I now shall grant each of you one wish."

Mom went first. "I want to travel the world with my wonderful husband!"

The fairy waved her magic wand, and instantly in the wife's hand appeared plane tickets and travel vouchers.

However, her 50-year-old husband enamored with the genie said, "Thank you very much for those tickets, but this is a once in a lifetime opportunity! I'm very sorry honey, but I want a wife 30 years younger than me."

The fairy waved her magic wand once again and immediately turned the husband turned into an 80-year-old man.

Do it mom's way. "If at first you don't succeed, try doing it the way your mom told you to do it from the start."

-- Anon.

Real-life. "Such an awful picture of both of us, but I love it! I love it because it's real life! It's not shot in any studio...we're not all gussied up in our Sunday best...heck, we couldn't even manage to fully open our eyes...life is silly and messy and beautifully imperfect. And it all started with this woman! Thanks, Mom, for being my best friend! I love all our moments together...picture perfect and otherwise!"

-- Carrie Underwood on her mom

Feeling guilty. "My mother could make anybody feel guilty - she used to get letters of apology from people she didn't even know."

-- Joan Rivers

Octopus moms and other moms in nature. Did you know these?

A mother octopus will guard and attend to her eggs for up to seven and a half months without eating (in the case of the Pacific Octopus). During this time, they guard their eggs against predators such as crabs and squid and the mother also squirts water on the eggs repeatedly, giving them oxygen.

The Emperor Penguin mom will leave her egg with the father and travel up to 50 miles to hunt for food and regurgitate it for their hatchling.

Polar bear moms stay with their cubs for two years training them to survive in the wild.

Elephant moms stay with their calves for up to six years.

Alligator moms carry their babies in their mouths to protect them from predators.

For the Mother Who Has Everything, Bruce Miller & TeamGolfwell

Mom feeds them. She feeds them when they are babies and then through most of their twenties."

-- Anon.

Give shoes away? Your uterus isn't the only thing that grows when you are pregnant. Your feet grow too up to a couple of sizes, so you have our condolences if you might want to give away some shoes. [24]

Please and Thanks

You taught me how to wash my face

And how to use the potty.

You made me eat up all my greens

And wiped my nose when snotty.

You taught me to say Please and Thanks,

Because politeness is the way,

So 'Please' can I borrow some money?

Thanks!

Just kidding!

-- Anon.

There's no tooth fairy. "You can't be the tooth fairy, Mom, since you always say you don't have any cash."

-- Unknown

Sound familiar? If you've ever read Goldilocks and the three bears, have you noticed that Papa Bear's beautiful porridge is hot, baby bear's porridge is just right, but Mama bear's porridge is cold?

Only at bedtime. Have you ever asked your child how school was today on the ride home and got no response?

Then at dinner, you ask if he or she had fun at school today and again, get no response.

Then you say goodnight at bedtime, and you hear, "Guess what happened at school today!"

Decisions. A dad gathered his family around to announce, "In this family, I am the General, and mom is the Major."

The children looked puzzled, so dad continued. "That's because mom makes all the major decisions, while I decide on the general ones.

Great moms. A good mother lets you lick the mixing beaters. A great mother remembers to turn off the beaters.

Momtini. One-part bubbling personality. Two parts God-like patience. And a tiny dash of a Wonder Woman.

Independence. A parent's definition of independence is what we want our children to be as long as they do everything we say.

Respect mom. (This is an old joke you may have heard) A teacher asked her young class to ask their parents for a family story with a moral at the end and to return the next day to tell their stories.

In the classroom the next day, Johnny gave his example first, "My dad is a farmer, and we have chickens. One day we were taking lots of eggs to market in a basket on the front seat of the truck when we hit a big bump in the road; the basket fell off the seat and all the eggs broke. The moral of the story is not to put all your eggs in one basket."

"Excellent," said the teacher.

Next, Mary said, "We are farmers too. We had twenty eggs waiting to hatch, but when they did, we only got 10 chicks. The moral of this story is not to count your chickens before they're hatched."

"That's excellent too!" said the teacher, very pleased with the responses so far.

Next, it was Harry's turn to tell his story: "My dad told me this story about mom. Before they got married, she was one of the first fighter pilots in the Iraq war and her plane got hit. She had to bail out over Bagdad and all she had was a bottle of gin, a machine gun, and a machete."

"Go on," said the teacher, intrigued.

"Mom drank the whole bottle of gin as she glided down, and she landed right in the middle of a hundred enemy soldiers. She killed seventy of them with the machine gun until she ran out of bullets. Then she killed twenty more with the machete 'til the blade broke. And then she killed the last ten with her bare hands."

"Good heavens," said the horrified teacher, "What did your dad say was the moral of that frightening story?"

"Stay away from mom when she's been drinking."

Irish proverb. "A man loves his sweetheart the most, his wife the best, but his mother the longest."

"I've done it before. Let's get this birth thing over with." The shortest time between two births is 208 days - approximately 6½ months. Jayne Bleackley gave birth to a boy on September 3, 1999. Then, she later gave birth to a daughter on March 30, 2000. [25]

The Interview. A young police recruit was asked during his interview, "What would you do if you had to arrest your mom?"

Without any hesitation, he said, "Call for backup."

I owe you, mom. "All that I am, or hope to be, I owe to my angel mother."

    -- Abraham Lincoln

The best. "My mother thinks I am the best. And I was raised to always believe what my mother tells me."

    -- Diego Maradona, an Argentinian and known as one of the greatest football players of all time.

Empty bottle. Mom says, "There, there. Don't cry, mommy cries too when her bottle is empty."

For the Mother Who Has Everything, Bruce Miller & TeamGolfwell

Relax, Mom. You've won.

As a mom you are number one

A parent who is second to none

On Mother's Day, chores you should shun

For it is time for relaxation and fun

Even if at the end of the day nothing gets done

Just remember we will still love you a ton!

-- Unknown

Weather. My mother taught me about the weather when she would say, "Look at your room! It looks like a tornado went through it!"

Be a lady. "My mother told me to be a lady. And for her, that meant be your own person, be independent."

-- Ruth Bader Ginsburg, US Supreme Court Justice

Tribute to his mom. "My mother said to me, 'If you are a soldier, you will become a general. If you are a monk, you will become the Pope. Instead, I was a painter, and became Picasso."

-- Pablo Picasso

Powerful. "There is nothing as powerful as mother's love, and nothing as healing to a child's soul."

– Unknown

Decisions, decisions. I once met a man who had been married for 50 years, and in this changing world today, I thought to myself that's amazing. So, I asked him, "What's the secret to such a long, happy marriage?"

"Well," he replied, "It's like this. The man makes all the big decisions... and my lovely wife and mother of our children just makes the little decisions."

"Really?" I responded. "Does that really work?"

"Oh, yes," he said proudly. "50 years, and so far, not one big decision!"

Heart of a mother. The heart of a mother is a deep abyss at the bottom of which you will always find forgiveness.

– Honore de Balzac

Stages of moms. At 4 years old a child believes his mother can do anything.

At 8 years, a child believes his mother knows a lot.

At 12 years, a child believes his mother doesn't know everything.

At 14 years, a teen believes that his mother of course does not know everything.

At 16 years, a teen believes a mom is old-fashioned.

At 18 years, a teen believes his mom is completely out of touch with the modern world.

At 24 years, a son or daughter has determined mom might know a little bit about it.

At 35 years, a son or daughter seeks mom's opinion about it.

At 45 years, a son or daughter wonders what mom would have done.

At 65 years, a son or daughter wishes they could have talked to mom about it.

Only a mother can say this, "No matter how much I say I love you; I always love you more than that."

– Unknown

Get it done. "There are three ways to get something done: do it yourself, hire someone to do it, or ask your kids not to do it."

– Malcolm Kushner

A fourth child. "You want to know what it's like having a fourth kid? Imagine you're drowning, then someone hands you a baby."

– Jim Gaffigan, Comedian

Get tough. "The strong mother doesn't tell her cub, son, stay weak so the wolves can get you. She says, 'Toughen up, this is reality we are living in.'"

-- Lauryn Hill

Don't touch. "It's weird, all those parenting books my wife made me read, and not one ever hinted that I'd have to remind my son not to touch the dog's butthole."

-- Jr. Williams, Comedian

Special Birthday present. "My mom always tried to make birthdays special for me. One year, she put a life-sized inflatable clown in my room, like it'd be neat when I woke up. Let me just tell you guys -- you don't know fear until you wake up in the middle of the night to use the restroom, and there in the darkness is what appears to be a man in a clown outfit, watching you while you sleep."

-- Isaac Witty, Actor Comedian.

Teacher. Mama was my greatest teacher, a teacher of compassion, love, and fearlessness. If love is sweet as a flower, then my mother is that sweet flower of love.

-- Stevie Wonder

From the Cat

I thank you for the food you bring,

and for my little squeaky thing.

I thank you for your friendly talks,

and when you change my litter box.

I thank you for the naps we share,

and putting up with tufts of hair.

I thank you for these things you do,

but thank you most for being you.

So as I'm sat upon the mat,

Happy Mother's Day from me the cat!

-- Unknown, but might have been written by the cat to the cat mom.

Mom is the hero. "When I wrote the book (Born a Crime), I thought that I was the hero of my story. And in writing it, I came to realize over time that my mom was the hero. And I was, you know - I was just her punk-ass sidekick."

-- Trevor Noah

Starting a fire. Mom knows but does not let on her knowledge that a 7-year-old boy can start a fire with a piece of flint while a 40-year-old man says it can only be done in the movies.

Mom's menu. "My mother's menu consisted of two choices: Take it or leave it."

-- Buddy Hackett

Favorite toy. Have you ever noticed that your child's favorite toy is the one they just lost?

Evolution. "If evolution works, how come mothers only have two hands?"

--Milton Berle

Newborns. "Parents of newborn babies are basically hostages in their own house with a severe case of Stockholm Syndrome."

-- Nate Smith

It's actually the house or me. "Both of us can't look good at the same time; it's me or the house."

-- Anon.

Puddle. The definition of a puddle is a small body of water that draws little clean shoes into it.

Notes in lunchboxes. "I'm totally 'that dad' who leaves a note in my son's lunch box. One day I'll actually start putting food in there also."

– Steve Ryan, Comedian

Mom's favorite chores. "My second favorite household chore is ironing. My first being hitting my head on the top bunk bed until I faint."

– Erma Bombeck

Instructions needed, please… As the nurse handed me my newborn she asked me, "You got this?"

I replied that at times "I have to dig through the trash to re-read the instructions for mac 'n' cheese."

The lightest baby. Little Kwek Yu Xuan was born via emergency C-section weighing about as much as a softball — just 7.5 ounces, or 0.4 pounds — making her by many accounts the lightest baby ever delivered. [26]

Before Kwek Yu Xuan, according to the Guinness Book of World Records, the next lowest birth weight was 8.6 oz – not even a pound. The baby and parents have kept their names confidential, and, in the United States, the baby was delivered by Caesarian section in San Diego, CA in Dec. 2018 after a gestation of 23 weeks and 3 days.

The tiny San Diego baby is back home, healthy and doing well. It was reported that Dr. Paul Wozniak, the physician who performed the Caesarian said the child's prognosis was bleak, and he said, "We weren't sure she would survive. It's been an honor to have been a part of the child's care team, and to have the privilege to watch her grow, thrive, and exceed all expectations." [27]

Religion. "My mom taught me religion whenever she would say, 'You'd better pray that will come out of the carpet.'"

Sleep Metaphor. "I don't want to sleep like a baby, I want to sleep like my husband."

-- Anon.

Barbara says you can do it. "Jeb Bush's brother Neil said that their mother has 'come around' to the idea of Jeb running for president in 2016. Because if there's anything that says you're qualified to be president, it's your own mom saying, 'I guess you could do it.'"

-- Jimmy Fallon

Blue or pink? Pink or Blue? Some families have a boy and a girl, some have two girls, some have two boys, some have all girls, some have all boys, etc. According to the Guinness Book of World Records the Ewers family of Chicago set a world record with 11 children in consecutive order of boy then a girl, boy then a girl, etc. in an extraordinary order in alternate gender births in one family. The eleven children who were born to parents Thomas and Katherine are,

Thomas B. Ewers (1955)

For the Mother Who Has Everything, Bruce Miller & TeamGolfwell

Marie Martin (1957)

David Ewers (1958)

Monica Jones (1960)

Michael Ewers (1961)

Paula Penn (1963)

James Ewers (1965)

Jane Christensen (1968)

Daniel Ewers (1970)

Katherine F. Ewers (1972)

William Ewers (1975)

Surprised very much they didn't run out of names. Is there any way to influence a baby's sex?

The short answer is no, according to the Mayo Clinic post as there's not much the average couple can do to affect a baby's sex.

"It has been reported that, "Deep penetration, for example, doggy style, means the male sperm that can swim faster start their race closer to the cervix and are more likely to reach the egg first, resulting in a boy.

"It's another interesting theory, but again there's nothing to support this idea. Dr. Michael Thomas MD (fertility specialist) actually advises that there are no methods to affect the sex of your child, including sexual position. [28]

No transition. "The biggest thing I remember is that there was just no transition. You hit the ground diapering."

--Paul Reiser, Comedian

Mom's arms. A mother's arms are made of tenderness and children sleep soundly in them.

-- Victor Hugo

"My mother is a strong woman. Her strength comes from being tested by life's unpredictability. It comes from soldiering on for her children, even when she might rather have given up. I know it hasn't always come easily, but I also know it's her greatest gift."

-- Matt Lauer

Odds of living longer. According to several scientific studies, mothers who give birth to their last child after the age of 33 have twice a better chance of living to 95. And, in general, mothers who give birth later in life have a better chance of living longer. [29]

Two Smiles. A woman has two smiles that an angel might envy, the smile that accepts a lover before words are uttered, and the smile that lights on the first-born babe and assures it of a mother's love.

-- Thomas Chandler Haliburton

Uh oh! When mom hears the toilet flush together with the little words "Uh oh!" she already knows it's too late.

Burnt out? I once read there was a mom who was complaining to her husband that she was feeling burnt out. Then she said her two-year-old grabs her cheeks and says, "Mommy, you should put on some sunscreen!"

More burnout. One mom swore that "Hell hath no fury like a toddler whose sandwich was been cut into squares when they wanted triangles."

Wake-up time. On Saturday mornings, the kids wake up around 6 am.

On Sunday mornings, they wake up at 5:30 am.

On Monday mornings, they wake up around 8:15 am and usually miss the bus.

Mom's advice – thank you! "When your mother asks, 'Do you want a piece of advice?' it is a mere formality. It doesn't matter if you answer yes or no. You're going to get it anyway."

– Erma Bombeck

Tree of love. "I love my mother as trees love water and sunshine. She helps me grow, prosper, and reach great heights."

-- Terry Guillemets

That's Italian. Good food and a warm kitchen are what make a house a home. I always tried to make my home like my mother's, because Mom was magnificent at stretching a buck when it came to decorating and food. Like a true Italian, she valued beautification in every area of her life, and I try to do the same.

-- Rachael Ray

Show-off. The definition of a show-off is any child who is more talented than your child.

Keep the teens at home. "The best way to keep teens at home is to make the home atmosphere pleasant and let the air out of their tires."

-- Dorothy Parker

First friend. "A mother is your first friend, your best friend, your forever friend."

– Unknown

Flexibility. Did you know during pregnancy you become more flexible? The baby gives you the gift of a gymnast so to speak. Your body releases a hormone called relaxin that softens ligaments and the tissue that connects joints. This makes your delivery easier. Some say this also helps you paint your toenails when your bump is in the way. [30]

Failing – here's a quick remedy. "Even on the days, you feel like you are failing, look around. Your child's smile will bring you right back up"

– Unknown

Overheard. My wife and I were taking several of our little nieces on a day trip and they agreed among themselves that Santa had to be real because their mom was "too cheap to ever spend that much money on a gift."

For the Mother Who Has Everything, Bruce Miller & TeamGolfwell

-- Anon.

What is sex? A joke. A little girl runs out to the backyard where her father is working, and asks him, "Daddy, what's sex?"

Her father sits her down and tells her all about the birds and the bees. He tells her about conception, sperms, and eggs. He goes on to tell her about puberty, menstruation and tells her the works. He covers a wide and varied assortment of subtopics and by the time he's finished, his daughter is somewhat awestruck with this sudden influx of bizarre new knowledge.

Her father finally asks: "So what did you want to know about sex for?"

"Oh, mommy said to tell you lunch would be ready in a couple of secs..."

Mom Koalas have odd ways that work. A mother koala will produce "pap" to feed her baby that contains bits of her own feces. Baby koalas—or joeys— who are born blind haven't developed the intestinal bacteria that help detoxify the highly poisonous eucalyptus leaves. The pup needs pap which contains this bacterium to properly digest eucalyptus leaves. Eucalyptus leaves are a koala's main diet. [31]

Dividing love. "For a mother is the only person on earth who can divide her love among 10 children and each child still have all her love."

– Unknown

A blender. "A two-year-old is kind of like having a blender, but you don't have a top for it."

-- Jerry Seinfeld

Sleeping in when you have children. That's when you lie in bed trying to figure out what that crash just was.

Being strong. "I think God made a woman to be strong and not to be trampled under the feet of men. I've always felt this way because my mother was a very strong woman, without a husband."

-- Little Richard, Music recording artist

A rock. "I am closest to my mother, as she is my rock, my pillar of strength, and my world. Not only has she stood by me through all times - happy, sad, and otherwise - but there have even been moments when I had completely lost hope, and her immense belief in me had lifted me up."

-- Amruta Khanvilkar, Indian actress

Leftovers. "The most remarkable thing about my mother is that for thirty years she served the family nothing but leftovers. The original meal has never been found."

-- Calvin Trillin

Respect mom. "The greatest thing a father can do for his children is to respect the woman that gave birth to his children. It is because of her that you have the greatest treasures in your life. You may have moved on, but your children have not. If you can't be her soulmate, then at least be thoughtful. Whom your children love should always be someone that you acknowledge with kindness. Your children notice everything and will follow your example."

— Shannon L. Alder, from "300 Questions LDS Couples Should Ask for a More Vibrant Marriage"

Definition of a sweater. "A sweater is a garment worn by a child when the mother feels chilly."

– Barbara Johnson

Positive. "My mother taught me to be honest, to be selfless, and to touch people in a positive way."

– Scott Eastwood, Actor

Good things happen. Scientists have theorized that the hormones that flood the brain during pregnancy can lead to permanent loving alterations in mothers, like the way teenage hormones contribute to adolescent brain development. [32]

Shower. "A mother need only step into the shower to be instantly reassured she is indispensable to every member of her family."

-- Lynne Williams

Peace. Mother's love is peace. It need not be acquired; it need not be deserved.

-- Erich Fromm

Perfection. "There's no perfect way to be a mother. But there are a million ways to be a good one."

-- Jill Churchill

Screwdrivers. Mom was putting together a new desk and she asked her 5-year-old son's friend Joey to bring her a screwdriver.

"Do you want a 'Daddy' screwdriver or a 'Mummy' screwdriver?" Joey said.

Confused, mom said, "Bring me a Mummy screwdriver."

Joey came back with a butter knife.

"I used to give my friends who have kids advice all the time, and they would look at me like I had three heads. And then, when I had two, I literally apologized to all my friends."

-- Jennifer Lopez

Sound familiar? A mom wondered if her 5-year-old has ADD since when she asks him to brush his teeth before going to bed, he regularly sling-shots his underpants into the bathtub.

Keep it secret. "My sister said once, 'Anything I don't want Mother to know, I don't even think of, if she's in the room.'"

-- Agatha Christie

Moms actually have 3 sets of eyes. "It's the three pairs of eyes that mothers have to have...One pair that see through closed doors. Another in the back of her head...and, of course, the ones in front that can look at a child when he goofs up and reflect 'I understand, and I love you' without so much as uttering a word."

-- Erma Bombeck

A mom with three daughters. One mom reported her mother had unique and different ways to get her point across to her three daughters who were close to the same age as they grew up. The girls seemed to constantly argue amongst themselves over everything including, of course, their favorite clothes…even if they hadn't worn them in years. Mom knew simply asking us to stop arguing didn't work and had her own ways.

For example, when riding a car and hearing the girls argue and shouting at each other "Shut up…No you shut up…Youuuu shut up…and so on,"

Mom would say, "HEY HEY…We do NOT say shut up in this family! WE say SHUT THE HELL UP!"

That made everyone immediately stop shouting, then a brief silence followed, then everyone would burst out in laughter with Mom teaching her girls valuable lessons through her magical and spontaneous sense of humor.

Man enough. "Still, I pulled her into a hug, because I knew she let me off the hook -- on purpose -- and yeah, I'm a guy and I love my mom. So, shoot me. I'm man enough to hug her without feeling like a mama's boy."

— Nyrae Dawn, from "What a Boy Wants"

You should write Chris. Christopher Columbus' mother is reported to have said, "I don't care what you discovered. You could have written."

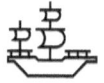

Just amazing! One boy in class said his definition of his mom is a person who has the amazing ability to hear a sneeze through closed doors, in the middle of the night, three bedrooms away… While daddy snores next to her.

Bottle feeding. What is bottle feeding? One definition of bottle feeding is an opportunity for Daddy to get up at 2 am.

Truest friend. "A mother is the truest friend we have, when trials heavy and sudden fall upon us; when adversity takes the place of prosperity; when friends desert us; when trouble thickens around us, still will she cling to us, and endeavor by her kind precepts and counsels to dissipate the clouds of darkness, and cause peace to return to our hearts."

Washington Irving (1783 -1859) Author or Rip Van Winkle and The Legend of Sleepy Hollow.

Mom has her back. "I can pinpoint that as the single happiest moment of my life because I realized then that mom would always have my back. It made me feel giant. I raced back down the concrete ramp, faster than I ever had before, so fast I should have fallen, but I didn't fall, because Mom was in the world."

— Maria Semple, from "Where'd You Go, Bernadette"

Motherhood is basically finding activities for children in three-hour pockets of time for the rest of your life.

– Mindy Kaling

Multi-task. A mother is a person who can carry a screaming toddler, two gallons of milk, talk on her cell phone, and still correct you for looking at her crazy.

The birth of a mother. "Giving birth is little more than a set of muscular contractions granting passage of a child. Then the mother is born."

– Erma Bombeck (1927 -1996) Humorist who achieved great popularity for her syndicated newspaper humor column describing suburban home life from 1965 to 1996.

A story behind everything. "But there's a story behind everything. How a picture got on a wall. How a scar got on your face. Sometimes the stories are simple, and sometimes they are hard and heartbreaking. But behind all your stories is always your mother's story, because hers is where yours begin."

— Mitch Albom, from "For One More Day"

Food cravings. During pregnancy, strong flavors can pass through amniotic fluid so it might be true when you joke that a baby wants what baby wants. When a strong food craving strikes during pregnancy, you may joke but there is some truth to "Baby wants what baby wants." [33]

Disappointed. Joan Rivers said this about her daughter Melissa, "The only time she really cried is when I sat her down and told her that she was not adopted."

Real love. "The only love that I really believe in is a mother's love for her children."

— Karl Lagerfeld, German creative director, fashion designer, artist, photographer, and caricaturist.

Fuel. "A mother's love is the fuel that enables a normal human being to do the impossible"

– Marion C. Garretty

"If I wasn't at work, I just wanted to stay home and party with my little man — and by 'party' I mean, of course, endless rounds of 'Itsy Bitsy Spider."

– Olivia Wilde

Boy or Girl? Scientists have studied pregnancy during the first and second trimesters and determined women are more apt to feel disgusted if they are carrying a boy. If you feel revolted over food, smells, and other things, you are probably carrying a boy according to a study done in 2015. [34]

A good job done. "But kids don't stay with you if you do it right. It's the one job where, the better you are, the more surely you won't be needed in the long run."

— Barbara Kingsolver, from "Pigs in Heaven"

3 am adventure. One mother reported that getting up at 3 am is of course difficult but it can be an adventure since if you think about it, at 3 am and you don't know if they are seriously ill or if their mouth feels spicy.

Mom's diet. Some parents say 75% of their calorie intake comes from licking spoons. Moreover, "It just occurred to me that the majority of my diet is made up of food that my kid didn't finish…"

-- Carrie Underwood

Silence. Silence is golden unless you have kids, then silence makes you suspicious.

-- Anon.

Most love. Moms are the people who know us the best and love us the most."

– Unknown

Actress. It's the best acting of my life right here, the well-rested woman. It's my finest role.

-- Kerry Washington

Best love. "The best love in the world, is the love of a man. The love of a man who came from your womb, the love of your son! I don't have a daughter, but maybe the love of a daughter is the best, too. I am first and foremost me, but right after that, I am a mother. The best thing that I can ever be, is me. But the best gift that I will ever have, is being a mother."

— C. JoyBell C.

Remember this one? "Don't open another box when there is a box already open." Plain and simple logic and wonder why it happens over and over. Must have something to do with unspoken freshness?

Definition of a mother. On the lighter side, a mother is a person who appears in the bathroom with a towel after you scream, "Mom!" three times when you're inside the shower.

"Mother is a verb. It's something you do. Not just who you are."

    – Dorothy Canfield Fisher

It's all basically simple. Motherhood is so much simpler if you stop explaining yourself to others and just do what works for you and your family.

    -- Anon. (i.e., don't compare yourself with others, and disregard comparing others to yourself)

Mother's Day – Don't feel bad if you didn't get any cards. A female salmon lays three thousand eggs a year and has yet to receive a Mother's Day card from one of them.

    -- Joan Rivers

Get a dog. "When your children are teenagers, it's important to have a dog so that someone in the house is happy to see you."

– Nora Ephron

Money well spent. Americans spend $14.6 billion on gifts on Mother's Day, including $671 million on cards and $1.9 billion on flowers. [35]

Ironic. "Being a mom has made me so tired. And so happy."

– Tina Fey

How to get the kid's attention. "The best way to get your children's attention is to relax and look comfortable."

– Anon.

Thanks around the world. "I wanted to take a second to just thank all moms around the world. Whether you birthed your children or adopted them, whether you're technically just a stepmom, whether you aren't raising your own, God had this plan for you. Thank you and thank you for always making everything better. Finally, thank you for challenging us to be better."

-- Ireland Baldwin

No manual. "Life doesn't come with a manual; it comes with a mother"

– Unknown

You can't quit mom. Your work is too important. To others, your work may not look like much, and I know it doesn't feel like much. But if you (and other mothers) quit sweeping the kitchen, nursing their bruises, and staging impromptu little tea parties along with the thousands of other things you do to enrich the lives of your children, the world would simply fall apart.

-- Unknown

No goodbyes. "There are no goodbyes, wherever you are, you will always be in my heart, Mother."

– Mahatma Gandhi

We hope you enjoyed our book!

If you liked our book, we would sincerely appreciate your taking a few moments to leave a brief review.

Thank you again very much!

> TeamGolfwell and Bruce Miller

About the authors

Bruce Miller. Lawyer, businessman, world traveler, golf enthusiast, and Golf Rules Official, actor, shrewd gambler, whiskey connoisseur, and author of over 35 books, a few being Amazon bestsellers, spends his days writing, studying, and constantly learning of the astounding, unexpected, and amazing events happening in the world today while exploring the brighter side of life. He is a member of Team Golfwell, Authors, and Publishers.

TeamGolfwell are bestselling authors and founders of the very popular 220,000+ member Facebook Group "Golf Jokes and Stories." Their books have sold thousands of copies including several #1 bestsellers in Golf Coaching, Sports humor, and other categories.

For the Mother Who Has Everything, Bruce Miller & TeamGolfwell

We Want to Hear from You!

"There usually is a way to do things better and there is opportunity when you find it." - Thomas Edison

We love to hear your thoughts and suggestions on anything and please feel free to contact us at Bruce@TeamGolfwell.com

For the Mother Who Has Everything, Bruce Miller & TeamGolfwell

Other Books by Team Golfwell and Bruce Miller

Brilliant Screen-Free Stuff to Do with Kids: A Handy Reference for Parents & Grandparents!

Inspirations

Dragonflies: A Novel Based on What Men Think of Women

The Funniest Quotations to Brighten Every Day: Brilliant, Inspiring, and Hilarious Thoughts from Great Minds

Jokes for Very Funny Kids (Big & Little): A Treasury of Funny Jokes and Riddles Ages 9 - 12 and Up

And many more here

For the Mother Who Has Everything, Bruce Miller & TeamGolfwell

Contents

Boring?...1

Mothers 1

Eagle eye. 1

Mrs. Germanotta's advice to her daughter Lady Gaga. 2

The influence of babysitters..2

Humbling..2

How true 2

Puzzling and funny 3

Mom's phone message left on her daughter's phone. 3

Where did she go? 3

An "exceptional" mom. 4

A clever way to get a wake-up...4

Stylish mom. 5

The better you are. 5

After birth...6

Glad that you're my mother 6

Lots of kids. 6

"You'll be fine,"..7

For the Mother Who Has Everything, Bruce Miller & TeamGolfwell

"Hey! Mother of five!" 8

Only one day off a year? 9

Supermodel mom 9

A mother's unusual dilemma 9

Tired mom: 10

Young moms choosing names 10

Helping God 10

Mi casa, su casa 10

"Nobel Prize for Mothers" 11

Driving with mom. 12

A mother's eyes. 13

"I am free." 13

A mother knows things no one does. 13

An easy birth? 14

Complicated stuff. 14

True story. 14

Automatic attitude adjustment. 15

A loving toast to mom. 15

Leonardo DiCaprio. 15

Can't get that stuff off easily. 16

Like mom like daughter. 16

Oldest Moms. 16

Realistically speaking 13

Changing diapers…help! 13

Thinking of having more than one child? 13

Unique. 14

Wait till the baby cries. 14

Thank you is not enough, Mom 15

Chinese Proverb. 15

"There is only one Mom." 15

It's time! 16

Show me. 17

Toddlers 17

Making room 17

How did Mother's Day begin in the US? 17

Cleaning. 18

Home Security 19

A child's eyes. 19

For the Mother Who Has Everything, Bruce Miller & TeamGolfwell

Dumbwaiter. 19

Amy got busy 19

Easy? 20

Be yourself. 20

What's this bill? 20

Silence 20

Best Mother's Day Present. 21

One-handed 22

What are you eating? 22

A mother's heart actually does grow. 23

Don't mess with mom. 23

Month of May 24

Sharing. 25

Joy. 26

Greek God 26

Cleaning your son's room 26

"Al, you must look good for the picture 27

The Silver Plate. 27

I marvel 29

Metaphor 29

Understanding feminism 29

Hi Mom! 30

You know you're a real mom when… 30

The first 12 months. 33

Steadfast prayers. 33

What does your mom do? 34

Voice tone is important 35

Record for heaviest baby. 35

A new perspective. 35

Male-dominated pastry 36

First Lady. 36

After they leave the nest 36

Cabby. 36

Transformation. 37

Bull####? 38

Mr. Rogers 38

The one and only Rodney 38

Oprah's view 39

Amy Schumer on birth. 39

No more bull####. 40

Hi mom!. 40

Cleaning house. 40

Frat house. 40

Dating the right man. 41

Only a mother knows this 41

Working moms 41

"I promise not to get angry". 42

Motherhood takes patience. 42

"I found life". 42

Tom Hanks. 43

Bad investment?. 43

Mom's influence. 43

A mother's wish. 44

First word 44

"Say Mama". 44

Think you know love 44

Full Heart. 45

"Everyone should have kids 45

Ideal Mom. 45

A mother's advice to her children. 45

The doctor is amazed 47

Roll with it 48

Men are necessary. 48

It's your turn. 48

Single mother. 49

A new role 49

Teaching your child 49

Guinea pigs? 49

Mom's humor through tough times. 50

Riddle. 50

Mom kept Christmas. 50

Saying no 51

Logical. 51

Selfless love. 52

Single moms. 52

Superior smells. 52

Want more than two kids?...52

Amazing 53

Don't be pushed around. 53

Said no mom ever. 54

How many?..54

Groceries..54

Roseanne. 55

Learn laughter. 55

Believe in yourself. 55

Great cook. 56

Prodigy? 56

What? 56

Feedback. 57

Immediate good behavior..57

Not easy. 57

Do I still have chores?..57

You trusted me and my crazy goals. 58

I took your advice mom...58

Never alone 60

Grandparents. 61

Magic Genie. 61

Do it mom's way 62

Real-life. 62

Feeling guilty. 63

Octopus moms and other moms in nature 63

Mom feeds them 64

Give shoes away? 64

Please and Thanks 64

There's no tooth fairy 65

Sound familiar? 65

Only at bedtime 65

Decisions 66

Great moms 66

Momtini 66

Independence. 67

Respect mom 67

Irish proverb. 68

"I've done it before. 68

The Interview. 69

I owe you, mom. 69

The best. 69

Empty bottle 69

Relax, Mom. You've won. 70

Weather. 70

Be a lady. 70

Tribute to his mom 71

Powerful 71

Decisions, decisions 71

Heart of a mother. 72

Stages of moms. 72

Only a mother can say this 73

Get it done. 73

A fourth child. 73

Get tough. 74

Don't touch. 74

Special Birthday present. 74

Teacher 75

From the Cat	75
Mom is the hero	76
Starting a fire	76
Mom's menu	76
Favorite toy	77
Evolution	77
Newborns	77
It's actually the house or me	77
Puddle	78
Notes in lunchboxes	78
Mom's favorite chores	78
Instructions needed, please…	78
The lightest baby	79
Religion	79
Sleep Metaphor	80
Barbara says you can do it	80
Blue or pink? Pink or Blue?	80
No transition	82
Mom's arms	82

"My mother is a strong woman 82

Odds of living longer. 83

Two Smiles. 83

Uh oh! 83

Burnt out? 83

More burnout. 84

Wake-up time 84

Mom's advice – thank you! 84

Tree of love. 84

That's Italian 85

Show-off. 85

Keep the teens at home 85

First friend 86

Flexibility 86

Failing – here's a quick remedy 86

Overheard. 86

What is sex? 87

Mom Koalas have odd ways that work 87

Dividing love. 88

A blender. 88

Sleeping in when you have children 88

Being strong 88

A rock. 89

Leftovers. 89

Respect mom. 89

Definition of a sweater. 90

Positive. 90

Good things happen 90

Shower. 91

Peace 91

Perfection 91

Screwdrivers 91

Sound familiar? 92

Keep it secret 92

Moms actually have 3 sets of eyes 92

A mom with three daughters 93

Man enough. 94

You should write Chris 94

For the Mother Who Has Everything, Bruce Miller & TeamGolfwell

Just amazing!..94

Bottle feeding...95

Truest friend..95

Mom has her back...95

Motherhood 96

Multi-task...96

The birth of a mother 96

A story behind everything 97

Food cravings...97

Disappointed..97

Real love...97

Fuel..98

"If I wasn't at work,..98

Boy or Girl?..98

A good job done...99

3 am adventure...99

Mom's diet...99

Silence..99

Most love 100

Actress 100

Best love 100

Remember this one? 100

Definition of a mother 101

"Mother is a verb 101

It's all basically simple. 101

Mother's Day 101

Get a dog. 102

Money well spent. 102

Ironic 102

How to get the kid's attention. 102

Thanks around the world 103

No manual 103

You can't quit mom 103

No goodbyes 104

We hope you enjoyed our book! 105

About the authors 105

We Want to Hear from You! 106

Other Books by Team Golfwell and Bruce Miller 107

Break out. 123

Feeling normal. 123

References... 124

Break out. "I love you so much my darling baby. But the minute your father comes home, I'm going to bust out of here like I'm escaping San Quentin prison."

--Anon.

Feeling normal. "After we got home from the hospital, I didn't shower for a week, and then John and I were like, 'Let's go out for dinner.' I could last only about an hour because my boobs were exploding. When the milk first comes in, it's like a tsunami. But we went, just to prove to ourselves that we could feel normal for a second."

-- Emily Blunt

References

[1] Wikipedia, https://en.wikipedia.org/wiki/Feodor_Vassilyev

[2] "World's most fertile woman who had 44 children by 36 stopped from having more babies". The Mirror. 16 October 2019, https://www.mirror.co.uk/news/world-news/worlds-most-fertile-woman-who-20589957

[3] Wikipedia, https://en.wikipedia.org/wiki/List_of_people_with_the_most_children

[4] Kickass facts, https://www.kickassfacts.com/mom-facts/

[5] https://www.guinnessworldrecords.com/world-records/oldest-mother-to-conceive-naturally

[6] https://www.guinnessworldrecords.com/world-records/oldest-person-to-give-birth

[7] https://www.guinnessworldrecords.com/world-records/oldest-woman-to-give-birth-to-her-grandchildren

[8] https://www.guinnessworldrecords.com/world-records/oldest-playboy-model

[9] HABAUSA, https://www.habausa.com/blog/10-mind-blowing-facts-about-mothers/

[10] Healthline, https://www.healthline.com/health/pregnancy/pregnancy-facts#facts

[11] Ibid.

[12] Ibid.

[13] Wikipedia, Anna Jarvis, https://en.wikipedia.org/wiki/Anna_Jarvis

[14] Ibid.

[15] Mayo Clinic Staff, https://www.mayoclinic.org/healthy-lifestyle/pregnancy-week-by-week/in-depth/pregnancy/art-20045977#

[16] Guinness World Records, https://www.guinnessworldrecords.com/news/2021/4/a-history-of-record-breaking-births-650288

[17] World Population Review, Maternity Leave by Country, https://worldpopulationreview.com/country-rankings/maternity-leave-by-country

[18] Great speech, https://greatspeech.com/the-babble-battle-why-do-babies-say-dada-first/

[19] Daily Mail, https://www.dailymail.co.uk/health/article-310627/Men-better-nappy-changing.html

[20] Web MD, https://www.webmd.com/baby/features/pregnancy-food-cravings-aversions#2

[21] Wikipedia, https://en.wikipedia.org/wiki/Multiple_birth

[22] Pew research, https://www.pewresearch.org/social-trends/2015/12/17/1-the-american-family-today/ and Insider, https://www.insider.com/the-average-number-of-kids-per-family-in-every-state-2019-2

[23] Wikipedia, https://en.wikipedia.org/wiki/Roseanne

[24] Livescience, https://www.livescience.com/27583-foot-size-pregnancy.html#:~:text=Pregnancy%

[25] Guinness World Records, https://www.guinnessworldrecords.com/world-records/67459-shortest-interval-between-births-separate-confinements#

[26] New York Post, https://nypost.com/2021/08/10/smallest-baby-ever-finally-goes-home-after-year-in-hospital/#:

[27] Supra at, https://www.guinnessworldrecords.com/news/2021/4/a-history-of-record-breaking-births-650288

[28] Supra at https://www.guinnessworldrecords.com/news/2021/4/a-history-of-record-breaking-births-650288

[29] TIME, Inc. https://time.com/2922235/mothers-birth-pregnancy-aging/#:~:text=The%20study%2C%20published%20in%20the,last%20child%20by%20age%2029.

[30] You and your hormones, https://www.yourhormones.info/hormones/relaxin/

[31] Save the koala, https://www.savethekoala.com/about-koalas/life-cycle-koala/

[32] Scientific American, https://www.scientificamerican.com/article/pregnancy-causes-lasting-changes-in-a-womans-brain/

[33] The Guardian, https://www.theguardian.com/lifeandstyle/wordofmouth/2014/apr/08/child-food-preferences-womb-pregnancy-foetus-taste-flavours

[34] UF Health podcasts, https://podcasts.ufhealth.org/pregnant-and-feeling-disgusted-you-might-be-having-a-boy/

[35] Fact Retriever, https://www.factretriever.com/mother-facts

www.ingramcontent.com/pod-product-compliance
Lightning Source LLC
Chambersburg PA
CBHW021427070526
44577CB00001B/98